MIRACLES OF THE SOUL

PERVIN VATANSEVER

BALBOA.
PRESS

A DIVISION OF HAY HOUSE

Balboa Press books may be ordered through booksellers or by contacting:

Balboa Press
A Division of Hay House
1663 Liberty Drive
Bloomington, IN 47403
www.balboapress.com
1-(877) 407-4847

Because of the dynamic nature of the Internet, any web addresses or links contained in this book may have changed since publication and may no longer be valid. The views expressed in this work are solely those of the author and do not necessarily reflect the views of the publisher, and the publisher hereby disclaims any responsibility for them.

The author of this book does not dispense medical advice or prescribe the use of any technique as a form of treatment for physical, emotional, or medical problems without the advice of a physician, either directly or indirectly. The intent of the author is only to offer information of a general nature to help you in your quest for emotional and spiritual well-being. In the event you use any of the information in this book for yourself, which is your constitutional right, the author and the publisher assume no responsibility for your actions.

Any people depicted in stock imagery provided by Thinkstock are models, and such images are being used for illustrative purposes only.

Certain stock imagery © Thinkstock.

ISBN: 978-1-4525-3307-0 (sc)
ISBN: 978-1-4525-3308-7 (e)

Printed in the United States of America

Balboa Press rev. date: 3/31/2011

APPRECIATIONS

Thank you God, for giving the strength and the inspiration to finish writing this book, and thanks for letting me to get together with my spiritual friends, who are currently reading these lines, in this life.

CONTENTS

A LETTER TO GOD

My Dear God;

I love you so much that the words we know in any language on earth cannot be enough to express it, besides I don't need the words to tell things to you. My thoughts and my feelings are already known and understood by you.

Before 2009, I had never written to you. Why? You already know the reason of it but I want to tell it in order to share with other friends. I have always been taught to pray when I am in bad conditions or if I do something wrong, I will be punished by you. Until recently, I have never thought that you would love me. Then I wised up and understood that you love all of us unconditionally very much. Now, I can almost hear you saying that it is exactly true. You are always with me; every day, every moment, when I'm happy or sad. I have always thought that there is me and you separately. However, I understand it now that you and I constitute a whole.

Actually, I am little ashamed of you, my God. Why? You already know I will tell in order to share. You created the world for us as full equipped to supply all of our needs and you gave us the power for being able to change anything we want with the newer and better one day by day. Unfortunately my God, some of us don't consider it as enough. In some areas of the world, there are people who die because of the starvation my God, but the others don't do much for them. In some places of the world, there are wars my God; people kill each other while the others don't do anything except watching. In many places of the world, human beings torture to the animals you created my God, and the others just ignore. There is so much anger, hate, war, blood, animosity and selfishness in the world so much that cannot be fitted in these lines. You already know but I will do, what I did many times on my own, now for the readers of these lines; on the behalf of all bad and badness, on the behalf of all cruel and selfish ones, on the behalf of the ones who are hooked on worldliness and just forgot you , the ones just mention your name without really mean it and even abuse your name, live in their own world; the ones don't praise, don't appreciate and say I am full you can be starved, pollute the earth, harm the environment I APOLOGIZE, I APOLOGIZE, I APOLOGIZE…

Please forgive us. You know that if there is a bird with a broken wing, I suffer more than the bird, and just as you taught us I help every living being as far as I could. I know that it is not enough. It wouldn't be enough to thank you even if I dedicate myself to serve for the universe. Anyway, I still endeavor. As you know, my life continues by helping the ones who need help, healing the ones who need recovery and shed light on people's life who needs leading. You know that, I will go on helping the living beings and serving the universe until the last breathe of my life, but for once again, in the presence of my siblings who are currently reading these lines 'I promise you!' that I will accomplish my mission which is the reason of my presence on earth. It is my only wish to accomplish my duty successfully and improve my maturity. When I come to the presence of you,

I don't want to bend my head down in front of you like guilty children. On the contrary, I would like to be on the presence of you with the tranquility of accomplishing my mission successfully.

Sometimes I am criticized and sometimes I am judged but as you know I never mind such things. I just do my duty and keep on loving you.

You know that, writing this book is the part of my duty, and while doing this part of my duty your angels are helping me. Serving for humanity is my mission and helping the universe is the purpose of my life.

What I am writing here is new for the readers while they are already known by you. Just as the sun rises every morning without any delay and leaves its place to the moon when the time comes, I am going to keep waking up every morning to do my duty until the time is up which you defined for me. For everything you have been giving to us THANK YOU VERY MUCH!

I LOVE YOU MY GOD

I LOVE YOU MY LORD

I LOVE YOU MY CREATOR

YOUR LOVING SERVANT

PERVİN VATANSEVER

INTRODUCTION

Most of you probably wonder what is going on in the world, like me. Surely, you are surprised by becoming true of all the fears and complications when you try to avoid them. All of these are utter results of the renovation of the energy around our world. It is like, recently all fears and anxieties have become true and all of us have been living maybe the most dramatic scenes of our lives. Yet, there is only one thing to remember in these conditions: Every difficulty, every experience makes the one more mature and nurtured. In other words, if I say it in spiritual language, the one turns into a 'light-laborer' by getting specialized on every field.

The reason of me writing all these things is to help supporting you on your own life journey and turn your fears and stresses into pleasure. Now, it is time to confront with the fear and complications. Not then, now. It is the very moment to convert them.

All these experiences are parts of our maturation. So, let all happenings happen as they should be, let experiences flow into your life; instead of being angry with life be grateful for all teachings. Believe in your faith; let water flow from the taps of the life, don't turn off the taps, don't afraid of cutting of the water. It never cuts off either the love of the Creator or the companion of the soul with us. Here or anywhere else, it doesn't matter. The Creator and we constitute a whole and we are always together. Let's touch to your souls now. It is the perfect moment.

THE MIRACLES OF THE SOUL

This book was written to share with you how we can contact with our souls and how we can create miracles by understanding our souls truly and getting in touch with them. It is possible to live the life you have desired by getting in touch with your soul. To succeed it you should learn how to look for the answers in yourself, be patient, act courageously and be connected to the center of the life.

Actually when a person improving his/her relationship with own soul, usually benefits from his/her own instincts, because our souls communicate with us through the instincts. As you read this book, you will transit into a life based on instincts and get in touch with your soul. When you communicate with your souls, you will be communicating with God and he is always with you, inside you. ☺

WHAT IS THE SOUL?

The soul is our own selves behind us which we know as ourselves. It knows and loves everything and is always in a progress. Don't forget that we are spiritual creatures which live humanistic experiences, not humanistic creatures which live spiritual experiences. The purpose of the soul is to reach accuracy and perfection through the all lives. Consequently, our lives will be full of love and happiness as much as we communicate with and understand our souls in this journey of life. Every requirement for us to be happy and able to love is inside of us. Don't look for it anywhere else, head towards in to you.

A JOURNEY INTO YOU

You can go on this journey after you find yourself a place where you can never be disturbed, switch the phones into silence mode and warn the people around you not to disturb you. First of all, lie down on something you can be relaxed and stay silent while listening to a calming music with your eyes shut. Just focus on your breathe and continue relaxing. When you inhale slowly, imagine that every breath you take approaches you to communicate with your soul.

Now, go towards to your secret shelter where you feel yourself special and secure. It could be a seaside, a forest or a mountain cottage. When you get there, feel the way it makes you feel, feel the colors flourishing and feel the sounds to render the place more real. This place belongs to only you and no one can come into, except you. Now, you are all relaxed. Ask a question about any part of your life which you are curious about. For instance: What should I do about my marriage? Or what are the things I should do about my job? … Etc. Just wait. Don't hurry and use your whole intelligence to percept how you feel. What do you feel in your body? What do you see? What do you hear? There is not just one way to get answers to those questions and of course, there is no one correct way of it. There is just your own way. When you get the answer, open your eyes and write down the answer immediately.

This exercise is the first communication with your soul and the starting point of your journey into you. Now, you are connected with your soul. That means that 'I don't know.' Is not an answer for you anymore because your soul knows every answer of every question. So, just communicate with your soul. ☺

IF YOU ARE IN A VICIOUS CIRCLE

If you feel yourself in a vicious circle, the first thing you must do is to change your focus. Setting positive focus is the safest way. For example; when you say 'I'm not afraid of the exam.' you focus on fear. Instead, saying like 'I can be successful at the exam.' does not just change your focus; it also gives message to the universe like 'this is what I want and I focus on it'.

Your soul knows all solutions for your problems and wants to inform you so much. Because it knows our life mission and it is in charge of helping us to make decisions for our life so, there is infinite information flowing from your souls to you.

Now, what you should do is to ask your soul what to do in order to get out of the vicious circle and distressing situation. You could do this as a meditation or just by staying at the usual conscious level.

What should I do?

What makes me happy?

What are the things I should change?

What do I need to be able to accomplish them? You can ask questions like these. Never force yourself to get the answer, just give yourself in your soul's wisdom. Don't forget that the instinctual insight which appears in your intelligence is always the best for you. ☺

THE HAPPINESS HUNTER

Most people complain about unhappiness while just few people ask 'how should it be the happy life for me?' and endeavour for it. Always remember that we are here, on this earth to love and be happy. A happy life is strongly correlated with your communication with your soul because your soul always leads you through the life which in tranquility, serenity and confidence always makes sense. Considering the instinctual messages accurately makes your life undergo in transformation.

Well, how can you differentiate that the instinctual messages coming from your soul are real or just your suppositions? It is so easy; the real instinct makes you feel the happiness, serenity, internal tranquility and infinite confidence. The information from the soul is filled with affection and comparison. You could check that if the universe says yes to you by regarding the clues I arranged below.

If you feel complete happiness, the message is from your soul. When something makes you happy you want to keep on doing it and this brings more happiness in to your life.

Focus on the question which asks how it should be the life that can make you happy. We frequently focus on the things we don't want instead of focusing on the ones we want so that we should change our focus.

Let's go to the life you have dreamed of. Close your eyes and imagine that you are living that life. Feel the moment and it has already started to flow more energy in to your life with this feeling... Be sure of that. Now, think about if there is someone or something that you can describe as an obstacle for you. Do you face any resistance? If you do, how can it be solved? Ask to your soul and keep on going. Be sure of that the universe has already received the energy vibrations which will present you your desired life.

You can access to the happy life of your dreams by inviting the events and people, which make you happy, everyday to your life, like that. It is enough to just want it. ☺

YOU AND THE ABUNDANCE

Human body is an electrical system which is enough for itself, produces by its own and we are ultrasonic vibrant beings. Every thought and feeling forms a vibration inside and around of our body. That's why you magnetize the ones which fit to your energy.

Usually, people focus on the missing things and this makes them more disappeared. It gets more negative when there are beliefs like 'I don't deserve it' or 'I'm not valuable' in the subconscious. However, you magnetize much more abundance in to your life when you are hopeful about yourself and your expectations from the life. First of all you should focus on the things which show that you are able to magnatize the abundance.

Now, close your eyes and focus on money. Imagine that money is flowing in to your life like it is flowing vigorously from a river and stay as you are. Live the moment and check out if there is any beliefs that decelerate or prevent the flow. Is there any?

How do you feel? Hopeless? Disappointed? Now, change the negative feeling into its opposite positive feeling. If you feel more happy and energetic, the operation is succeeded.

If you repeat this process every day for a month, you can attain incredible consequences and can announce your friendship with the abundance to the whole universe.☺

THE DEEP-FREEZER

Has there been any moment in your life that everything freezes like in a deep-freezer? Have you ever lived a period of life that seems like nothing happens? Actually, it is known as the discontinuation period and it is the messenger of the nice, happy and abundant days that will come afterwards.

During this period, you can learn so many things going on in your spiritual world by conforming to your soul and you can ask for help for your patience.

Have you ever seen a plant which blooms prematurely? Or have you ever heard them saying 'I have been waiting for days, nothing happened.' Of course you didn't. They wait for the right time, bloom when the earth is warm and sun is shining and present us their beauties. Your lives are just like theirs. The period in the deep-freezer is a preparation period for the next stage. Well, then praise for the period in the freezer and prepare for the next stage.

Now, play meditation music and close your eyes. Wait until you are completely relaxed. Go to your shelter which is your secret place once again. You are covered by a marvelous affection and confidence the moment you come into the place. Feel the energy and brightness. Wait for a group of guides to come near you and guide you by answering your questions about this period. Here they are; now you ask them whatever you want and listen to the answers carefully. Ask the most important question at the end: 'What am I supposed to learn during this transition period?' When you get the answer, ask them for help and thank them. When you are ready, reach to the usual conscious level and write down your answers. These are the answers of your soul for you. Don't worry and trust to the answers and be sure of that you didn't make them out. The important thing is the content of the information not the source of it. If this information makes you calm, feels you in safe and screaming that it is useful for you, nothing else matters. Enjoy it. ☺

LIVE THE MOMENT

When we really understand that, our time on earth is finite and we don't know when it is going to end, we start to live everyday savouringly as it is our only day. Unfortunately, even now, when you are alive, you always think about the next step and always plan the things you are going to do in the next moment. Because of that, you always miss the 'now' or 'this moment'.

If you are complaining about it, you can change this just right after reading this writing. Do you know how? Starting from right now, start to spend ten minutes regularly everyday by just feeling the moment. Just feel the energy and glamour of that moment. After carrying out this process regularly for few days, there will be incredible changes and you will start to live the moment with an increasing awareness day by day. This process is your outcry to the universe saying 'I deserve to spare time for myself and catch the glamour of the moment; I am worthy of it and I live it.' You are wonderful. Now, it is turn for the life to watch out itself. ☺

SAYING FAREWELL TO THE FEAR

We can't escape from the fear but we can say farewell to it through our instinctual guidance we can attain from our communications with our soul. Sometimes, you want to make, little or big, any change in your life and it excites you. However, after a while you feel glow of fear about the alteration and the fear is usually a sentence which begins with 'What if....' At this very point, making some changes might seem like a hard and depressing thing to do. That's why, you should proceed step by step and you should praise yourself for every step you beat the fear. Because, when you start to take small steps, success will bring more success and you will more self-confident and courageous.

Now, close your eyes and relax. When you feel completely relaxed, ask your soul-your spirit what you are supposed to do about your any fear. Wait. When you are convinced that you got the answer, get back to your usual conscious level and consider the answer.

You can consult with your soul about any subject that you feel frightening and distressed about it. Taking a courageous step every day, makes you feel like a million dollars. Remember that you cannot escape from the fear because it doesn't stop following you as long as you don't say farewell to it. Well then, say farewell to it, you don't need it anymore. ☺

YOU AND YOUR DREAMS

We all know that dreams are the way to correlate with the spiritual world. Dreams help us to solve our problems, make decisions and choices and discover ourselves.

Dreams guide us with some symbolic images. You could be consulted through your life mission by your dreams and can study on it. As far as we spend most of our time asleep, not benefiting from our dreams seems not so sensible. Does it?

We see that interpreters split into two groups about interpreting dreams; some says that dreams are unspecific while the others believe that dreams are specific that I think all dreams transmit special message for its dreamer. Your dreams transfer the spiritual messages from your soul to you, and according to me considering the messages is the one's privacy.

It is crucial to remember the spiritual communication with your soul -your dreams- since all dreams come with its unique messages. That's why it would be really useful to keep a dream diary, and also after a while you would have prepared your own dream guide book.

To be able to get spiritual guidance through your dreams, ask questions about the situation you want to get guidance before you fall asleep. But be careful about not asking optional or multiple choice questions. Ask questions with clear answers. Then, fall asleep and if you don't get any answer at the very first night please don't sink into hopelessness. It is possible that your soul wants to answer your question during the next day by another technique instead of by dreams. Be patient. The answer will arrive sooner or later. Believe in the progress.

Pay attention to your feelings during your dreams because they play a crucial role during considering the dream and the anticipated case. Besides, the feeling in reality is usually the same with one of the feelings in the dream. Have a nice sleep. ☺

PRAYER ADDICTION

How beautiful is praying, right? It is so good for the soul. I have always thought that praying is essential for the soul as much as eating is essential for the body. Prays feed our soul like foods feeding our body.

Actually, praying is giving your problems into God's custody. Certainly, there are some difficulties in your lives which give you pain and distress. These distresses could be about health or money or maybe about your discussions with your spouse. If the problem has been the part of your life for a long time, you have probably tried so many things to solve it. Did they work? I hear you saying no. Well, then now, try this for a whole week:

Relax and close your eyes. Cool down slowly and take a deep breath. Then, give the problem you have been making an effort on it in to God's custody and say 'I couldn't handle with my .... problem which has been in my life for a long time and I have tried everything to figure it out. Now, I am leaving it to your spiritual power. I am completely surrendered and trusted in you through this process.' After that, you have nothing else to do besides waiting hopefully and patiently. Believe in that the solution will come in the perfect time with all its perfections. Before you come back to your usual conscious level, think about and pray for everything you have in your life.

Repeating that exercise for a week will provide incredible benefit about the destruction of your problem. But don't forget to be receptive for all information which can come through after this meditation. It means that you are in 'on' mood not 'off'.

When you pray faithfully, there will be absolutely a response. ☺

BEING DECISIVE

When you are sitting on the fence, you feel yourself in a bottomless pit. You make a decision but after a while you begin to confront with a dilemma about it. For instance; 'Is my marriage going to be okay or should I break up before I get damaged?' or 'should I keep working at my current job or looking for another one?' These are some dilemmas which may retain you from your sleep for nights.

The main reason of your dilemma is to seek for the safeguard of your decision. Human beings want to know the future and become indecisive. Probably, you heard of people who say that they can't decide or you have said exactly the same for many times. Yet, also being unable to make decisions is a decision itself.

Then, what should we do? How could our soul help us about making decisions?

If you listen to your soul, it will guide you step by step through your all crucial decisions.

Don't wait everything to be perfect to decide, because it will never come true. There will be always difficulties and obstacles. On every decision you make, the universe will support you. Making decisions will put it in move. The universe helps you more if you know what you want.

What you should do now is to set 2 solving options about the situation you can't decide on. Firstly, imagine the 1. option you set. Then repeat it for the 2. option. And then, listen to your soul. The one you feel happy, flexible and active about is the right choice. Be sure of that because your soul is never wrong. ☺

CONNECT TO THE ANGELS

In all Holy Scriptures the angels are mentioned as delegates between God and people. The angels are celestial beings that communicate with you by feelings, sounds, physical senses and sometimes by images.

As it mentioned in The Koran, every person has two angels and they are always with us from birth till death. The angels don't intervene in to our lives unless there is an emergency. First, we should ask them for help to receive help from them. Don't forget that they never intervene unless you want them to.

I met my protector angel in my sleep and met Michael, one of the archangels, when I am completely awake. Seeing and feeling their presence was awesome.

You can communicate with them whenever you want too. Do you wonder how? Take a sheet of paper and a pen and sit down silently. Remain as you are and imagine yourself getting within a blue cloud. Feel that you and the cloud constitute a whole for a few minutes. Focus on your hearth, now your angel is beside you and you are surrounded by a circle of affection. Ask your angel anything. As an answer, you may feel a sense and realize that words are forming in your intelligence. You can extend this process as much as you want and find all replies you have been looking for. When your questions run out, thank to your angel and write down your answers. Don't be afraid, you are not making them out. It gets easier to communicate them when you do more practices. Remember that this communication is priceless because the angels bring us the love and peace from the celestial world.

THANKS THEM ALL. ☺

ARE YOU AWARE?

Time passes quickly, doesn't it? Days, weeks, months and years pass through in a hurry like they are in a competition without a backward glance, and usually what we do is looking behind it.

Do you ever think of the passing years? Do you ever ask "Where was I, where am I? or How was I, how am I? " Or are you one of those who just let time to pass away? Now, take a break and think of your passing life. What is going on?

After this retrospective thinking exercise, because of we generally choose to ignore our successes, we-human beings usually remember the sadness and failures. Then again, the sadness covers our whole body, we bewail passing time and we let ourselves fall down into the dirty waters of the desperation sea once again.

Yet, there have been not just miseries in our lives. Even in the most dramatic scenes there are always huge miracles for the ones who really look and want to see. But the awareness is the initial condition. It really is, because before you notice, the time takes away the happiness just like it takes away the misery.

Now, I am asking:

Are you aware of the color you add into the world with your presence?

Are you aware how many lives you brighten up with your presence?

Are you aware how special you are?

Are you aware how valuable you are?

Are you aware how much you are loved?

Are you aware that you got a soul?

Are you aware for how many people you are unique?

Are you aware? You are alive…

Thinking, considering and making these sensible is your number one duty as a human. If you are not aware of all of these and keep living just by breathing, it doesn't matter for you if the time passes quickly or slowly, if it leaves a mark or makes a wound, if you are in a desert or in a flower garden. It doesn't matter at all. But don't forget that if it supposed not to matter, you wouldn't be here at all. You would have already gone to the place where you would notice when you are there. ☺

DANCE WITH THE MOMENT

How can one dance with the moment? You all always in a mad rush and hurry; but for being able to dance, you supposed to stop for a moment and coordinate with your partner. It means that, to be able to do that you have to focus on the moment. Now, take a deep breath and don't hurry when you are reading these lines, because you are about to change your life style and nurture a new awareness. Don't waste it, please. Act like in the Zen poetry: "I am sitting in silence, doing nothing. Spring comes and grass grows on its own."

To catch the moment, close your eyes for a few seconds. Stay as you are. Then, open the window and look out of it, take a deep breath. Combine with your soul and focus on it. You have already started breaking the pattern. You have just achieved to catch the moment by just thinking about this moment, not the past or the future. You can celebrate yourself. Take a deep breath again. Stop focusing on your regular works and enjoy the moment. ☺

HOLD ON TO YOUR DREAMS

In the universe, everything starts with dreaming. Because, after you dreamed about something, in a while it takes part in your life, and it could be as big as the person's dreams. Why has everybody got different dreams? Have you ever thought about it? They are all different because dreams are the messages coming from your soul and they give you the clues about your life aim and mission. As you know, you all have different souls so, you all have different dreams.

Humans dream more when they are kids. Especially if the one lives in a country, like Turkey, after a while gives up his or her dreams. The dreams are considered as useless and impossible in the complexity of the life.

But now, it is the time for you to change; commence to watch out your dreams. Consider your dreams as a spiritual guidance which will take your life to a better level.

Now, think back about your childhood and figure out which dreams, that you imagined back then, you have made true. How did you achieve it? In what did you believe in? How do you feel about it right now? Please, note them down. Then, this time think about your current dream or dreams. What are you supposed to do to live your dreams? Which steps you are ready to take? You may ask more questions to your soul. Please, write these answers down too. If there is a correlation between your childhood dream and current dream, it is a message from your soul. If there is not don't be upset because that means your soul need something new. Come on, dream. What are you waiting for? ☺

TOWARDS THE CONCLUSION

Every day, we make new decisions and want to add new things in to our lives. Sometimes you can quickly head towards to the conclusion where as it can take a long time or you can never be able to achieve it. Actually, the formula for achieving your desired conclusions is so simple. You may find yourself heading towards the conclusions rapidly when you are able to combine your goals and imagination, and include plenty of positive feelings and instincts in to the combination. The formula is so simple, and I must add that it is like a recipe. The meal would be savorless if you don't put every ingredient enough, and it would be useless.

First of all, you must set an accurate and really clear goal. After that part, many people get hung up about how they can attain it. Now, you put this issue into the freezer for a while. Just dream, feel positively and listen to your soul. How would you feel, when you reach your goal? Imagine yourself living that moment. Let yourself to your soul when you constitute a complete whole with love and the power which will lead you through your goals. After this stage, your soul will guide you via your instincts. During this process, don't do things because you have to, just trust your instincts. Your soul will transmit you the feelings required for your reaching to your goal. Every day, spare time for attaining your goals and be nourished by positive sensations. For all this time, keep your receivers on 'on' mode, and watch out every type of instinctual guidance that you may face with.

Watch out sudden insights, physical senses and strong happiness feelings. Don't worry about afterwards; the universe will handle with the rest for you, at the right time in the most appropriate way. You just dream and surrender. Reaching the goals will be much easier for this time, just believe in that. ☺

DON'T BE AFRAID OF THE ALTERATION

Are there any situations that you feel like you have to bear just because you are afraid of altering or trying something new? I guess, the answer is 'yes' for most of you. In that case, it could be beneficial to understand the reason of these situations first. People are frightened of changing because the same one gives trust and people always stick in to the situations they feel safe, like sticking in to a swamp.

Even if it is a predicament, this is the way the system processes. Because of your fear of changing, you create a flower garden in your life and get stuck in the outside of it, in the dissatisfaction part.

My advice, to all frightened ones, is looking in to your own eyes in the mirror and say the word 'alteration' every morning after you wake up for ten days. When you are saying it, observe your body. At the beginning, your muscles will be convulsive but day by day they will be relaxed when you are saying the word. Then, keep doing it when you are also doing little changes in your life. For instance, drink coffee instead of tea or tie your hairs up for one day if you usually loose them. Including new things into your life and get good reactions from the people around you will not just change your point of view to alteration, but also be the first steps of your next changes. As you all know that the only thing which doesn't change is the changing itself. Especially in these days, you, the ones who are in the universe, give up waiting for 2012. Never forget that as long as you change and become happier, more affectionate and more peaceful, dear angels will help you and the universe will be rewarding you for your achievements. You all deserve it, then start taking courageous steps towards the alteration without wasting any other minute. You can do this. ☺

WHY 'ME'?

People usually ask this question when they encounter with a bad situation. Actually, there are some anger and even some hatred in this question, because the situation is though, painful and also insoluble for them. They think that they don't deserve to be in such situation. But still, every bad situation has a message and a meaning under its cover. When you encounter with an undesirable situation, just ask the 'why me?' question and back off. When you are doing this, leave your anger and offenses aside. How could it be if it wasn't like that? Why did it happen? How can I turn it into positive situation? Why me? The answers you are going give these questions will make the situation more clear for you and will help you to replace the negative and painful feelings with positive ones.

You should always remember that there is always something to learn from your experiences and it may not seems like it is right to experience it now but be sure of that it is the best time.

Never forget that noble God created a wonderful universe and everything processes perfectly in it. Sun is rising in the mornings and the moon appears at nights in the infinite sky. As you see, when everything is going unbelievably well, in the meantime everything lives their maturation; the universe, you and me, everything. No matter how you consider it, every experience is required and essential for your maturation. Who knows what kind of awards and gratitude there is for your soul when you sigh about your experiences. Remember that we are here to figure it out so, the next time you ask 'why me?' don't forget to thank God. Who knows what gifts, how beautiful awards are hidden in it for you. Don't you believe?

Then, look in to it again… ☺

FLIRTING WITH THE HEALTH

The health is the beginning of everything. Everybody mentions about the health, yet they choose the unsoundness. How? Of course, by keeping the negative thoughts and stress, which invite the diseases, in their intelligence. According to me there is only one type of disease and it emerges differently in all bodies. Since you are the ones who create illnesses, you can also create the healthiness. The intelligence and the positive thoughts it includes, are the essential parts to be able to handle with an illness. As long as you don't want to, even a single illness can live in your body. At the moment you decide to recover, the disease starts to pack its stuff. Because it knows that it cannot live in here anymore. When you focus on the diseases, they start to take bigger parts in your life. Even the diseases, which you consider them as genetic, are invited by you just like your parents did. And this reality makes your belief more strong. Your genes just settle down the occasions which are expected to happen. It is your choice to live them or not. You choose to live every experience in your life with the help of your both conscious and unconscious beliefs.

Now, it is time to flirt with the health. Every person is responsible and here for his or her own life. Once you decide to be healthy, nothing can prevent it yet, the universe never lets it.

The very first rule of flirting with the health is being grateful and it fills you with an incredible energy. Rule number 2; forgiving. I hear you say that it is too hard. Remember that God forgives every one of us despite of all of our mistakes so; we can forgive each other too. Rule number 3; remind yourself frequently that you are healthy. This reminding will contribute to the functioning of your cells. Rule number 4; laugh a lot because laughter is the best friend of the health. And, rule number 5; surrender. Surrender to the universe and let yourself in to the fluency of the life. When you surrender, your life starts to get full by the health coming all around.

Have a healthy day. ☺

THE CUPBOARD OF LOVE

Each of us born with an infinite capacity of love. Our hearths which are described approximately as big as our thumps are able to love unlimitedly. Unfortunately, because of the present life conditions and materialist approaches most of the time you forget this ability. As long as you forget, it become more stuck in and everywhere overflows with people who forget to love or remember to love a little. Sometimes, we wonder what do people love. There have been always the loved and not loved ones. Actually, if the one wants, can love everything. It is enough to just want. I want to remind that all of us born with an infinitive love inside of us and we have been always covered by the infinite and unconditional love of God. You can either remember this and live the life with full of love or just forget it and commit yourself to lovelessness.

Now, I want to share with you a method, which I frequently resort to, for the ones who demand to meet again with the ability of loving infinitely.

Choose a cupboard in your home. From now on, this cupboard is 'THE CUPBOARD OF LOVE'. Now, stand in front of the cupboard and say 'love' for 5 times before you open it. Then, open the door of the cupboard and close your eyes. Stand here and wait for a while and feel in your whole body that you are covered by an infinitive love. You will feel a wonderful happiness and peace. You can open your eyes and shut down the door when you think it is enough for you. How do you feel? Isn't it great?

From now on, whenever you feel like you need love or feel yourself loveless and exhausted, come in front of the cupboard of love and fill yourself up. Don't forget that eyes looking full of love and a hearth beating with love will always counsel you during the wonderful way of life. Stay with love in full of lovely days. ☺

GOODBYE ANXIETY

Saying goodbye to something or someone makes people upset, and causes sadness, but saying goodbye to the anxiety causes opposite effects. You invite the anxiety in to your lives. Your ego loves being anxious so much, but your soul doesn't love it at all. Human beings are always anxious; always find something to concern about. For the things haven't happened yet but are expected to happened in the future. People don't know that they bring the issues they have concerned about in their life with their anxieties. Then, they become addicted to the anxiety. They presume a simple headache as an implication of a brain tumor. They turn every little detail to a huge problem. By acting like that, they make the life miserable for their own and for the people around them.

Now, it is time to become clean from the anxieties and say them goodbye. Lie down where you cannot be disturbed and close your eyes. Take a deep breath and relax. Now, imagine yourself on a stone bridge which has a river flowing vigorously under it. Watch the river flowing under you for a while. Then, remember the things make you anxious and throw each of them to the river. Don't hurry and throw them away slowly until they are all gone. When water takes all the anxieties away from you, feel the peace and percept how though it was carrying all of these anxieties. Feel you are all relieved. Let them all go through the river because you don't need them at all. Don't be surprised how light you are without the anxieties on your back. When you are released of all unnecessary heaviness your soul is dancing; the reason of the happiness inside you is the goodbye dance of your soul to the anxiety. Now, invite the hope into your life and believe in it. Hopeful and confident life is on its way to you. Open your eyes whenever you want. Goodbye anxiety to never meet again. ☺

LOVING THE ONES YOU DON'T

Is there any one or ones you don't like? Is there? Then, it is time to change it. As long as you think of not loving, you turn your body into a negative-energy-ball. When you focus on the behaviors that you don't like or support, you cause them to be acted much more. Criticizing people usually make them vicious and make harder to change their behaviors. Flattering the people's behaviors that we like is the easiest way to make them act in the way we like. Flatter the one you don't like very much when he or she does something you like. Beside, ignore the behaviors you don't like. Most of the people give response to flattering more than they give to criticism.

Another way to love the ones you don't is to express what you want clearly. Ambiguity brings dissatisfaction. If you don't express yourself clearly, the consequence might be disappointment, because everybody has distinct perspective about every subject. A kitchen which is not cleaned properly for you may be considered as squeaky cleaned by your maid.

Now, think of a person or a situation you don't like. There is a poster which is written 'I don't love you.' on it in the one's or its hands. Its face is upset, isn't it? Slowly come closer to it and imagine that you are telling what you want to say, what you don't like, want you want to change, clearly. It is listening carefully and as you keep telling, the sadness on its face turns into smiles, right? Now, change the 'I don't love you.' poster with the 'I love you.' one. Lastly, cover it completely with a light and leave it.

Don't forget that everything deserves to be loved, so that they were created.

I love you so much. ☺

TAKING OFF THE SOULS' CLOTHES

I am speaking to the precious and full of love souls of you which are captured in a body and are under the influence of the ego and external world. I completely understand and respect you so much. You are full and complete, and we neither accept nor are aware of how we are torturing you when we maturate together. I know that our internal world-our soul and spirit- is so strong and no matter how though the situation you are in, you will find a way to turn it into goodness. You feel yourself depressive, anxious, afraid or like have lost the purpose of the life when you are disconnected with your souls. At just exactly that time you say 'my soul is bored'.

Before make you more bored, I invite you to relieve your soul. Now, connect to your soul and think of being in a communication with it. You are all relaxed and relieved.

Your soul is right in front of you but you can't believe what you see. Your soul is overdressed and it is almost choked. It is overdressed with sweaters, pants, coats and furs. The clothes are referred to sadness, anxieties, pains, sorrows and distrustfulness. Now, start to take them off one by one. But don't hurry and don't hurt your souls. Take off your souls' clothes. So that, they can be free and you can communicate with them. Think that your soul is relieving step by step and thanking you to remember and give it a chance to live. How are you? Do you feel eased? Great! I knew that you could achieve it. So now, hug your souls and say them: "come on naked souls, get back to the work, to climb up the stairs together through the maturation. ☺

RIGHT HERE, RIGHT NOW

Why do we constantly have dilemmas, feel sad, anxious and hopeless? Why do we always restrict ourselves and the others with pressures? Why can't we just be happy? Because, all the ways we were taught to reach the happiness nourish us with desires, feelings and actions which will actually reach us to the unhappiness.

We always make a list of the things we need to be happy because we have taught that we can't ever be without them. For instance, an employee works in a company thinks that if he had such a company one day, he would be happy. As you see, happiness is always correlated with an incident that must be achieved in the future. Is the owner of the company really happy? Or does he make requirement lists too?

Think of any necessity for you to be happy. If there is anything you can do right know, do it; so that, the energy that you waste by complaining constantly can be spent for a more positive purpose. If there is not, why do you waste your energy by complaining and sorrowing? The unique thing you should remember is that everything is about "right now, right here." Unnecessary sorrows, concerns and feeling yourself inadequate are just deprive you of the happiness and cheer you could live. If you are happy and full of love, no matter what the conditions are, no matter what people think or say, you can enjoy the every moment of your life.

Now, take a paper and a pen. Write yourself a letter which expresses the beauty of being right here, right now and tells you that you already have the requirements you need to be really happy. The future is formed with the conditions which have already existed, and when you discover how to live the happiness of being 'right here, right now', you won't need to be worried about the future. Live the moment and be happy right now. Live tomorrow when it is tomorrow. Don't forget that you just need yourself to be happy, the rest is not essential. You just be right here, right now. ☺

LOVE UNCONDITIONALLY

What is 'loving unconditionally'? It is just loving. Loving unconditionally is loving and saying "I love you as you are. I love you for being in my life journey. Even if we are completely different, I love you because our essences are the same, and the most important thing is I accept you as you are and don't want you to change."

Unfortunately, we have never taught how to love unconditionally. I love what is useful for me, not the useless one. I can love you more if you change these but if you still the same I don't. It is not unconditional love, it is love based on conditions. The real love is to accept the one as he is and also being able to view the life from his perspective.

First of all, we must learn how to love ourselves with all of our sins and merits. No matter how much mistake we did in the past, we should always love ourselves unconditionally. Just like the God loves us. When you learn how to accept and love yourself, you become closer to your spirit and spread higher vibrant energy.

How can you love the others if you don't love yourself? When your love to yourself and your love to the others become integrated you can be full of love.

Now, lie down comfortably and relax. Then, visualize yourself and say 'Dear me, I love you as you are, I accept you as you are. Don't be regret for the things you have done because I love you. We can't change the past, but we can live the future with love. From now on, always remember that God loves me unconditionally and I love me. I love me, I love me, and I love the world.' Stay as you are as much as you want. You will feel wonderful and covered by love when you get back to the present.

I LOVE YOU, no matter who you are, no matter what you have done, no matter which religion or nation you are from I accept you as you are and I love you. ☺

CHANGE THE PROGRAM

Does your life pass through in the garden of anxieties, sorrows, concerns, failures and unhappiness? If your answer is yes, that means your program is wrong. In other words, low level conscious programs are loaded into your brain and because of you live with this program, misfortunes never stop following you. Conscious programs include the programs which were loaded into our brain until we are 5. When you realize that you are complete and awesome and the only problem is the program you have been using, your life will undergo miraculous changes.

Well, how does this low level conscious program originate? For example, you are a 3 years old kid and you are playing with the lighter of your dad. Then, all of a sudden your dad comes into the room and takes it from you after yelling at you. You cry, you are afraid, you are ruled over, and your childhood passes through as being always under control. So, you were settled a program based on controls and rules, and you have been living like that. Until this day, of course, because now it is the time to change the program.

Lie down and close your eyes. For now, visualize three things of your disturbing or making life harder features. Add 'change the program' button next to each feature. Let's say there is 'I am concerned' feature, click on the program changing button and imagine it is being replaced by confidence and tranquility. You can practice this exercise as often as you want. After the exercise, write down the features you changed, keep your receivers open in the following days and note down the changes you will be making about that features.

Don't hurry, the alteration will come slowly. You just apply it; the universe will be doing the other miraculous alterations for you.

I hope you enjoy your new program. ☺

YOU ARE NOT A ROBOT

Have you ever felt like a robot which is programmed to do the same things every day? Are you one of those who keep doing what they have to do and ignore the voice raising from their soul and saying enough. Have you ever thought that if you don't let it you don't live like a robot? I hear you asking: 'if I don't do the things which have to be done, who will do?' I don't tell you not to do must-be-done things, I just suggest you to do them by respecting your soul's rhythm instead of doing them like a machine.

But how can you respect to your soul's rhythm? First of all, you must commence with understanding your soul's rhythm. To conform to anything first you need to get know it. The rhythm of your soul constantly sends you instinctual messages but you usually ignore them and keep acting like a robot. At this point you should just listen to your soul. You should ask: 'what should I do first?', 'how fast should I do it?' Then, of course, you shouldn't forget to add actions that are good for your soul and make you feel enthusiastic when you think of, into the must-be-done actions.

For instance, you are in a hurry. You have to pick your child up from the school and you are already late. When you are at the garden gate of the school you realize the woman who sells flower. You want to buy flowers but you are in a hurry so, you just pass through. That means that you deprive your soul of the beautiful colors, fragrant scents and the pleasure of the flowers. You act exactly like a robot and go towards to the school. However, just 20 seconds you spent for taking flowers could add beauties you haven't realized before to your life and may relieve you so that you can spread fresh energy to your child.

As you see, the choice is yours. You can either choose to live like a robot or live like a human being who listens to your soul and deserves the happiness and pleasure. Which one do you think you would choose? ☺

QUARTER TO MIRACLE

What is miracle? Where does it happen? When does it happen? Do you believe in miracles? Have there been any miracles in your life? Think about it...

The miracle is a situation which is not completely possible, so close to impossible and makes the one incredibly happy when comes true. In case of you believe in and want to, of course.

Now, think about the past and try to remember how many situations you have experienced that you can consider as a complete miracle. I can see the big smile covers your all face when you think about them. The miracles are awesome, make you walk on the air.

The miracle is a shift and processes in 5 steps.

1. You look at so many things around you but you don't actually see them. You automatically like the objects and people or deny them. First, you should learn how to look and see. Don't forget that nothing is like how it looks like. To live the miracle set yourself into a frequency you can perceive the miracles.

2. You must realize the distinction. That means, to be able to realize the incidents you let into your life you must perceive the differences like radar.

3. You go under the influence of the negative feelings like anger, sadness, nerviness you have been feeling less than before. Because you perceive them as stones you stumble on during your journey to your miracle. So, you pull them off the road and keep going on your way.

4. Your loving and espousing feelings begin to rise up because you are aware of that there will be a miracle real soon. So you keep waiting as you conform to the fluency.

5. You comprehend that you are the master of your own life, open yourself to the situations and people that may add beauties into your life, and let the others be tangent to your life.

When you accomplish all of these, you perceive that your life takes on new and good dimension, and understand that the miracle you are waiting for to happen is actually your creation. The biggest miracle is happening right now, right here. When you create your own miracle you also give a chance to the world to experience another miracle. Don't be away from miracles. ☺

WATCH YOUR OWN MOVIE

All the world's a stage,
and all the men and women merely players.
They have their exits and their entrances;
and one man in his time plays many parts...

Shakespeare

It is really how it is, isn't it? All the world is a stage and you are the leading actors of your own movies. The script, the cast and every other detail depends on you, choices of you. All of us play new roles again and again every day. Sometimes as a son, a mom, a teacher at a school, a spouse at home, an aunt of a kid or a grandson of someone. The scene and roles change hour by hour, that's why some who took parts in our lives in the past years are not here anymore.

Now, I want you to watch your own movie as an external viewer. Get off the stage and watch what is going on and how many parts of the scenario you create and act consciously. Is your movie a tragedy or a comedy? Determine the things you like or you want to change in your movie while you are sitting on the audience chair with the confidence of being an audience. As a scenarist of the movie you can do any changes you want in your new movie. You are also the leading actor so; you can remove the parts you don't want to act in. Add into your movie anything you want maybe more happiness, hope, imagination, awareness. Add more of the things you consider as not enough and remove the things you find so much or unnecessary.

This movie is yours. Nobody can tell you what role you are going to play or interfere in the scenario. It is your movie. Let's create your new movie and live it. You all deserve academy awards. Enjoy it. ☺

EVERYDAY, ONCE AGAIN

The life restarts every day! Doesn't it? Every morning is like a rebirth-pure and hopeful. The one should wakes up with gratitude every morning and be grateful for being still alive.

But, how many of you do it? How many of you leave yesterday in the past and enjoy today, the new day? We always start the new day as wrapped in quilts with the anxiety and fear of the tomorrow. Yet how meaningless and unnecessary is being anxious about tomorrow. Have you ever seen a bird which worries about finding food tomorrow and stock up food for tomorrow? I have not. Because all created living beings, except human beings, know that the God created their daily shares too. If it is distributed equally there is enough of everything for everyone; as long as we are aware of it and live accordingly. Leave yesterday behind. You learn from them and keep going on your way. Don't let yesterday, anxieties and sorrows follow you like a shadow. You are here because you all deserve to start over every day.

To be able to start over to the life every day, write this down in to a piece of colorful paper and stick it on to your bathroom mirror. Read it the minute you enter the bathroom every morning and feel it. Let the new day begin not just physically by waking up but also mentally by being grateful. Let it, so that all beauties which are already on their way to you don't give up when they confront with the anxieties of the yesterday and tomorrow. So, the way of the love, happiness, peace, confidence, success and joy to you is always be clean and without any stone and be decorated with flowers.

Since the life starts over every day, from tomorrow on, let it starts over together with me. Maybe someday, our ways intersect with and we say to each other; "don't forget life starts over every day." Who knows? ☺

DON'T UPSET THE WORLD

Hey you, my spiritual friends who are currently reading these lines, do you know that whenever you are hurt or sad, the world gets upset too. Believe in me about it. The world says "I do my best to make human beings happy but unfortunately I can't prevent them to be sad" and gets upset more than you. None of us has right to hurt the world.

Why are we here? Of course, we are here to learn. But, are all learned ones good and cheerful? Of course not. Some of them hurt us so bad, so deeply that we feel so alone, so desperate and like a victim. When you feel in this way, the vibrant you spread to the world will be at the same frequency. Therefore, you and the world get involved in each other's vibration and it feels all the sorrow of you but cannot do anything about it.

Isn't it the main stuff? You will learn with the pain, you will learn with the happiness; in every case you will learn. Since this is the way it is and since you are here then, let's delete all the past sorrows of the world.

Now, lie down comfortably and relax. Set free your whole body and intelligence and visualize the world in front of you. "Dear universe, from the day I started to live on you I might have hurt you or made you sad on purpose or not, but as you know we all have been learning. Now, I apologize for all the pains and sorrows I gave you in the past. I have always considered you as an un-living thing, but now I am aware of that you breathe just like me. Please, forgive me! I thank you for the oxygen you have been providing, for all blessings, for all the plants which colorized my life every season with different colors, and for your hospitality to all animals which love me unconditionally! I know that if you didn't exist I wouldn't exist too. THANK YOU!

As long as you do this exercise you will be full of the positive creative energy which strolls around the world, and become real friends with the world. Best regards to the world. ☺

GIVE ME MY FREEDOM

Sometimes our souls scream like that. They feel so stuck and imprisoned…

You mostly ignore this scream; act like it didn't exist and maliciously keep living your life which its freedom has given. If you say 'I don't understand how I could destroy my soul's freedom', this text was written for you to understand it and set your soul free.

A soul declares itself by making you feel meaningless internal boredoms if its freedom has taken away. When you think of, there is not any change in your life but you get bored because your soul gets bored. Your life is based on the notions and actions you consider as must be done instead of the ones related with your life mission. Then, you start to wander around with constant anger, like a ready-to-explode bomb. Because, your soul you haven't set free, leads you to live angry life. In other words, most of the times you feel like you don't belong to where you are. From time to time you say that your body is here but your soul is not.

If you face such things but don't know the reason of it or how to solve it, you have to understand that you should give your soul its freedom back.

But, how? Now, lie down comfortably and make yourself all relaxed. Visualize a white pigeon. Look at its face. How it is? Is it happy? Is it sad? Now put it in a cage carefully without hurting it. How is it now? Is this white pigeon-your soul more upset now? Observe its wings. It is flapping cheerfully, isn't it? Comprehend the messages, which the pigeon is transmitting to you, clearly and save them in to your intelligence. Now, slowly open the door of the cage and wait. When your pigeon-your soul is leaving say to it; "I am giving your freedom back to you and I accept all of your messages into my life and choose to continue to live my life with them."

Can you feel how relieved are you? Give your soul's freedom back to your soul because it is your freedom. ☺

THE GLOVES OF THE HELP

Helping is giving their needs to the ones who are in need of. Helping is not just one of the major facts of our religion, but also one of the features of being human. A person becomes more spiritually rich and full of peace as long as he helps. However, the humanity is in such a period and such things are going on all around the world; the people are so engaged with secular values so that they usually choose to ignore the people or any living beings, that are in need of, instead of helping them, and eventually they pay its price with their in-pain soul even without noticing.

Sometimes we see the ones who criticize the helpful people. For example, when a helpful person is struggling to help a starving dog, cat or a bird, the people around say him to help a person instead of animals that much. But we should ask to those people; "At least I am helping this living being. What about you? Who do you help except yourself?" Why are we here? To live together and give the things we have to the others who don't have. Just like noble God gives us everything, we should help the others. Unconditionally and from our hearts. Helping is also good for human health because when you help, the peace you feel in your soul directly affects the rhythm of your hearth so; the energy in your body flows and strolls easily.

Now, I have a suggestion for you. When you wake up tomorrow morning, promise yourself to open your life to help and to take active roles in every situation which will require any help, during the day. Then, visualize yourself wearing a couple of gloves (you decide the color). Today exist in the life as a person with his helping gloves. Spend the day and in the evening write down the helps you did that day and the reactions in your soul and your body. You are surprised by such beautiful consequences, aren't you? It is just one day but happiness and the feeling of complement is like you have been trying for months.

You can wear your gloves and try to make this world more beautiful whenever you want. You and your gloves. ☺

WHERE IS THE HEAVEN?

According to all Holy Scriptures, the heaven is a place where we can go to after death if we deserve to and it is full of beauties which we can never imagine. Reaching that wonderful place, where there is happiness, peace and infinitive love, is the main purpose of each of us. But is it necessary to wait until death to live the heaven? Cannot we start living the heaven when we are here by filling our lives with love, understanding, resignation and espousing? I think we can but we have to desire it and then go into action.

If you want too, let's go on a journey to the heaven in your intelligence. Lie down and close your eyes when you are not disturbed. Just wait and don't push yourself too hard. After a while your dream heaven will appear in front of your eyes. Copy it exactly in to your intelligence. Then, imagine yourself taking a walk in the heaven, wander around slowly with your protector angel. Ask anything you want to your angel without hesitation but don't forget to ask this question: "This place is so wonderful but I am in the world right now and I have to be there for a while. What should I do to feel the same way in the world?" After finish asking all of your questions and get the answers, don't forget to thank to your angel for its help and guidance during this trip.

Now, let's get back to the present. You have learned the ways and tricks of living the heaven in the world. The only thing you have to do is to apply the things you have learned from your angel to your life. The rest will be solved.

Remember, the heaven is in everywhere you are in.☺

GOD LOVES US

God loves each of us unconditionally, no matter what we have been doing and he is always so close to us. Actually, he is inside of us. Sometimes things happen in a way like he is responding our prays, and sometimes it looks like he didn't hear our help requests. When our lives are like that we think that God is disregarding us or he is mad at us, and we perceive the incidents as a punishment. But the truth is that God never disregards us. Actually, we are the ones who disregard him because we usually remember him to demand help when we are desperate. Then, can you please tell me, who is the disregarding one?

Most of us have disconnections in their relationship with the noble Creator and suffer because of that. The fact is that the reason of this suffering is not God; the reason is ourselves and our explanation of God. Because we see God as a punisher and interrogator as a result of the way we have taught. But when we understand him, we get that he is guiding us with love, not waiting for us to punish.

You can speak to God whenever you want, about whatever you want; you can even write to him. He is always with you, just don't disregard him.

He sees the love under the all of our sayings and actions. Even if we talk to him with angry voice because of the things that happened or didn't happen, he sees our loving face because he knows all of us better than we know ourselves.

After all, we are human beings created by him and came to the world to experience and learn. When we learn, he always watches us with love and supports us.

God is the only intelligence in the whole universe so that our intelligence is the same with his. He is at everywhere, in everything. If you can't notice the guidance of the God that means you fell apart from him, and you feel yourself so lonely. Remove these thoughts and feelings from your life immediately and don't forget:

God loves us, forever, forever and forever. ☺

THE BIG PICTURE

What is the 'big picture'? It is the main plan that contains the whole universe, which includes your life too, and it explains the situations we can't understand during our maturation journey. The things you have learned, the people you have met, and the pets which have taken part in your life, your experiences are all related with each other in some way. But we usually have difficulties in relating them with each other and we sometimes can't achieve it while we are experiencing them. However, after a while, we can see the interaction between them when we are able to see the bigger part of it.

For instance, imagine that there is a 1500 pieces of puzzle. When you put together the 15-20 pieces from the right corner, a tree comes up. Then put together some pieces from the left corner, this time a house comes up. For now, they look so irrelevant and so separate. But when you completed the puzzle these 2 irrelevant things will constitute a landscape picture with includes the house and trees in a forestland.

As you see the things which seem like irrelevant are actually directly related with each other.

Well now, how does learning this information provide me benefit? If you ask like that, here is the answer: If you don't perceive some situations you have been through and ask yourself questions like 'why does it happen in that way?' my advice for you is to follow your soul's guidance without hurrying up. When you go through by such periods, watch out the people you meet with, be careful about the things happen around you and just surrender and wait. Be sure of that, the right thing for you will become a part of your life at the right time, in the right way.

After a while 'what is the connection?'s will be replaced by 'so glad it happened's. You might demand all explanations immediately. But you can only attain the explanation with the appropriate speed and quantities. Otherwise, it may cause a complication. You are given as much as you could perceive. Knowing that there is a bigger picture of what we see, makes the one curious and gives hope, doesn't it? Who knows how the big picture is? I think it must be awesome, what do you think? ☺

THE FOUR MIRACLES

How beautiful is birth? It is a totally new beginning, clean slate. Every newborn living being are at the beginning of everything, who knows what is he or she waiting for? For happiness, for disappointment, for joys or for deepest sorrows. Births give both happiness and excitement. Here is such a story.

One day, when I came back to home from work, one of the street cats which I feed every day, bring me its 4 newborn kittens. Then I thought about the birth for a long time. It had cleaned the kittens and had put them side by side in front of the door. And the cat was little nervous, it trusted me but it was also anxious. Just like us, sometimes we trust and also think if there will be any damage, just like that. First, I was a little surprised and worried because I hadn't looked after a kitten before. Then, I started to think that there must be a message in this experience. Of course, when I was thinking about the message, I made a very beautiful nest derived of box for them and placed it in a secure part of the house. Then, I started to observe them by enjoying and trying to understand the teaching of the situation.

Then one day, when I was observing them again, their shaking trials to stand on their legs and trying it again fearlessly after every falling attracted my attention. And that day I perceived the lesson they were trying to teach me. I learned that even if I fall for hundreds of times during the life game I should try over and over again fearlessly, like I never fell.

What about you? Do you give up when you crash to the obstacles which make it harder to achieve the goal? Or do you try fearlessly like my little miracles?

I named the mother as marmalade and thanked to her. Why? For trusting me enough to choose my house as a home for her precious kittens she loves more than herself and reminding me the unconditional love by disregarding herself and struggling for her babies to feed them. Then, I thanked to the kittens because of their 'never give up, keep trying like every trial is the first one.' message for me.

Nothing is actually like how it looks like at first sight. Now, you review your life and things around you too. Maybe there is a message you haven't seen or couldn't see before. What do you think? ☺

I AM FULL AND YOU?

How deep people get caught up in the game, lies and the dream of this life. They say just me and always me. My family, my loved ones etc. so they forget that me is you and you is all of us. Their eyes are so blind by the shiny colors of the 'me polish' that they don't care about the rest.

Everybody prays and asks God to give the ones who don't have too. But how many people thinks that is God the only one to give them and do you do things for them or should you do? I think after every meal, I am full but what about the others? The kid who sells handkerchief in the streets, a dog looking in trashes, a cat meowing for the smell when you are frying the fishes. Are they full too?

Actually, there is two option; either 'I am full, do you want the rest' or 'I am full, I will eat the rest tomorrow'. Choose...

Now lie down comfortably and think of a person or a living being you wanted to help but you postponed for many times. Relax completely and imagine yourself feeding him.

What do you offer? What reactions does he give? How do the reactions affect your body and more importantly your soul? Feel all of them deeply. Then thank to him. Instead of he is thanking to you, you thank to him to give you the chance to live and remind you to say we not me...

I know that you feel peaceful, relieved and awesome. So, what are you waiting for? Make this imagination real. Don't forget we can reach to the light the day we say or we can say we instead of me. WE not me. ☺

DANCE

When did you dance for the last time? Or has it already passed from you? Or don't you feel yourself happy and joyful enough to dance? Why?

I think you answered the all questions. Dance is so good, isn't it? When you dance with all your hearth, your whole energy discharges and then recharges.

Now I will advice you an exercise which will be a secret between me and you. I want you to spare some time for it that you should be alone at home and are not disturbed. Now, you are alone at home and you have butterflies in your stomach because you are about to dance crazily with your favorite song. Just like, you did when you were child. If you want to sing too I suggest you strongly to get a microphone for yourself. Now, play the music and start to dance. Continue dancing in front of the mirror when you are thinking how funny and beautiful life is. There is no time limitation for this exercise. You are completely free. Dance as long as you want, in the way you like. How happy is the child inside you, right? This is the life!

After this practice you will not just feel relieved you will also realize that some actions which seemed to you so hard before you started to dance are not such horrifying. Then just try what would you lose? Just try and have fun. ☺

WHY AM I HERE?

Really, why are we here? To be successful, be a mom, be a teacher, go on trips, eat…? Or are we here for a more important reason and to accomplish a special mission?

Every life has a noble purpose underneath of its visible living because every human being comes to this world with a unique contribution. The main purpose of all of us coming to this world is to accomplish our maturation and to serve humanity during our own journey. When we are serving to the rest of the humanity, at the same time we carry out our maturation.

In order to get more clear information and insights about this:

Lie down and close your eyes. Call out to your soul and request it to show you a symbol which symbolizes your maturation. Wait silently. What is the symbol? Now, imagine yourself embracing this symbol. Visualize yourself brightening yourself and the others when you are carrying out your maturation with this symbol. How do you feel? Now, take the symbol in your hand and place it on to your hearth. Feel that you and the symbol constitute a complete one and whole. And say like that: 'right now, I choose to endeavor for the maturation of my own and other people toward my noble purpose. Pay attention to your feelings and your soul's sayings. With this exercise, you have just filled yourself with a complete new energy and set your new energy settings.

Determine the courses you enjoy and be good at in your regular life because these are the courses which will do the biggest contribution to your maturation. Don't force yourself to deny doing these activities, just surrender to your soul and never forget the reason of you being here.

You are so special and your presence in here, right now is so important and essential for the world so that, you are here! I LOVE YOU. ☺

THE CONTAGIOUS ANGER

Most people emphasize the importance of being calm but they can't achieve it. The physical damages to the human body that are caused by anger and nervousness are so much, that permanent anger is suggested as the main reason of the most diseases. Well then, which one are you? The angry one? Or the calm one? Or are you one those 'depends on the situation' people?

When people are angry, they wander around and between the negative energy levels and the energy fluency in their body has cuts. Keeping the anger permanently in your body causes some energy obstructions in the body. Then you reflect it and magnetize the qualm to yourself. Your perception closes and you can't exactly understand the sayings and also can't express yourself clearly. So, you don't just become an angry person but also become a noncummunicable person.

Negative frequency energies are like contagious diseases and infects from one to another very easily. For example, a man argues with his boss, and then he scolds his wife when he gets home. Then, the woman admonishes her child and the child kicks the cupboard in the room. This is how the system processes.

Now here is an exercise to calm you down. Imagine the person you are angry with and say to him or her 'I am so mad at you' for 5 times when his or her image is in front of your eyes then, continue with 'I am angry at you' for 5 more times. Now, your anger slowly begins to leave its place to calmness. Say 'I am trying to understand you' for 5 times and wait. What is happening when you are saying like that? Observe carefully. At the end, say 'I am making calm room for you in my life'. You can open your eyes whenever you want. I am glad you feel much better.

You can do this exercise as often as you want, for every situation you want. Trust me it is so useful. I make this exercise with my angry counselees and get really positive results.

The anger never stops following you because you feed it but you can leave it behind easily. Because you don't need it, and calm life is much healthier. Hope you live peaceful life, to nerveless days. ☺

THE BACK SIDE OF THE CURTAIN

We usually deny seeing the facts as they are, and judge, compare and cover them by appraising through our values. It is like drawing a veil over a window. You actually know that there is a window underneath the veil but you don't want to see it.

But, why? Because the fact is usually not the same thing we want or expect. So, we create a new illusion by adding our feelings and comments to the situations.

When we just look at the cover of something without examining it and don't go beyond what we already saw, all we can see is just an illusion. For example, you judge the people with their physical appearances before getting to know them. Judge and criticize the person if he or she doesn't fit to the image in your intelligence. If we enlarge the situation with another example; we describe a bagger or a homeless we come across at the street as pathetic because of the position we see him in and because of we couldn't see their real role. However the only thing we should do is just open the curtain and try to understand and see the reality underneath it. The situation he appears in front of us is correlated with his own maturation. We shouldn't describe the people by just looking at their current position. We should try to see the underneath of the curtain. But, how?

First of all, we must start with the fact that every person is here to accomplish their own maturation. Then you understand your own realities and act through your instincts coming from your soul. When you start to see under the curtain, you will become spiritually stronger and start to live miraculous experiences.

Now, take a few deep breaths and relax. Then visualize yourself and commence to discover yourself without judging. Focus well on your features you like or don't like, you are good at or inadequate at. Then, say to the universe 'I choose to see and understand the soul of everything. I am ready to know everything with their realities.' and wait. Feel the openings of the all curtains during this waiting duration. Congratulate yourself for achieving it and feel the joy.

From now on, you will start to live more brightened days by trying to see things with all their clarity and this is really a wonderful life. ☺

THE SEA OF THE MIRACLES

The sea brings salt to some people's mind or brings the water, swimming, the blue and many other things. But it is beautiful and peaceful and it gives hope when it is reflecting the sun lights.

But, what is the sea of the miracles? How can we reach there? And what can be done there? Do you wonder? Then let's go together.

Lie down comfortably, close your eyes and inhale deeply. Feel that you become more relieved and relax with every breath you take. Then, imagine yourself at the side of an infinitive sea. The weather is warm, the sand is hot and you are at the seaside. The sea invites you in it with all of its calmness and tranquility. Imagine yourself going in to the sea slowly. Feel the heat of the water. After few more steps let yourself go into the water and start to swim. After few strokes think about one of your impossible dreams and imagine it is coming true. Don't hurry and stroke out for few more times, this time think of an object that you would never afford for it and feel it. Keep swimming and after a while imagine yourself living the most successful and happiest moment. And wait. I know that you feel awesome right now. Now start to swim back to the seaside. When you get to the shore you can open your eyes.

You have just met the sea of the miracles and you have swum in its wonderful and sparkling water. Actually, the sea of the miracles is always inside you but you always see it as an impossibility and feel yourself never ready to go inside it because of the hesitations like; what if I get drown, what if it is cold. However your soul which is also your power, you desire, your determination and your guide, is looking forward to help you. You just let yourself into the water of the sea of the miracles-into the arms of the life. Just let yourself without any fear or hesitation but with trust and confidence. And, get little wet, what would you lose? Getting wet when you are trying is much better than living with the fear of getting wet. Isn't it? ☺

GIVE UP FOR YOURSELF

Most of us live for other people, not for their own. Who are them? Of course the ones we love most. Why? Because they are our indispensable ones and they are more valuable than us.

The love is such a strong and binding feeling that sometimes we discard ourselves, without even noticing, for the ones we love so much that we can't discard. During the life, we don't realize actually how heavy responsibilities they are for us. But the fact is; they don't put this heaviness on our shoulders, they don't ask us to be our indispensables, on the contrary, we place them in to the indispensables category and carry them. For example, a mother disregards her own life for the behalf of her indispensable child. A mother does sacrifices of course, but eventually this dispensable bag on her back makes her hunchbacked, makes her unhappy, depressive and sick. Yet, if she can keep her indispensable in a healthy relationship of love, not as heaviness on her back, she wouldn't have any weight or illness…

But, how we can give up of people for our own good?

Lie down, close your eyes and relax. Visualize a car of any model and color you want then, get in to the driver seat. Then, one by one, visualize 3 of your indispensable ones and slowly watch them coming through the car and getting in the back seat of the car. These 3 people must be so valuable and indispensable for you. Inhale slowly and after you are sure that doors are closed, start the engine and go on the road. Keep going with any speed you want for a while. After a while you will see a sign writing 'GIVING UP VILLAGE' on it. Here it is. Stop the car next to the sign and help them getting out. Hug them and say 'I love you but I am giving up your responsibilities for my own good'. Get back in to the car and when you are turning back the same way you came, wave your hand to your 3 indispensables from the mirror. Feel the relief and freedom inside you.

Don't forget that indispensables make you sick; the most loved ones make you healthy. Choice is yours. Either give up for yourself or get sick for yourself. Who can intervene? ☺

YELLOW ROSES

How beautiful are flowers? They are full of meaning and add colors in people's life. How much the one gets happy when receives a flower. Sometimes a flower bouquet is more valuable than an expensive present for the receiver.

Everybody has a favorite type of flowers. But the roses are always special, especially the yellow ones.

The yellow roses are both sadness and joy; they both make you look and pat, they also take you away and take you back.

When did you buy flowers for the last time? Do you buy flowers for yourself or just complain about not receiving any? Cannot a person buy flowers for him/herself? Why? Do you think actually he\she can? Well then, when did you buy flowers for yourself? Can't you remember? So, it has been a while.

If the person looks just outside for the beauties, the one either run into them so rarely or so late or never. All beauties must begin inside the person so that they can spread to the outside. So, today go outside but not for accomplishing the duties, just for you. Go to a flower store or ask the florist child on the street if he has yellow roses. Then buy yourself a bunch of yellow rose and write 'I LOVE YOU…' on a card. Take your flowers and turn back to home. Put the roses in to a vase. Make yourself a cup of coffee or tea and sit in front of it. And think about your first love, first disappointment, first graduation, first time you missed your dad, first goodbye to your mom, your first successful and anything else you want…

I hope your life will be always as beautiful as yellow rose gardens and I hope that yellow roses will always be your hope on your life road. ☺

TAME LOVE

The Creator had put love in every living being he created. Some of them show it on every occasion like cats' and dogs' whisking. Some of them look like cold, actually they love too but they don't snuggle. I call this unconditional love, that the way pets love us, as 'tame love'. Tame, because it is harmless, real and sincere.

But, how is the love that we, people give them? Tame? Harmless? Is it love or hate?

Every person loves loyalty and the loyal friends of us, dogs are the evidence of it. They love us forever. They love us even we yell and get angry at them; even we take away their life areas and imprisoned them in to the concentration camps that we call as shelters. They love forever because they know something we don't know and want to know. They know what? The unconditional love. Your cat or dog never looks for a reason to love you. They love you if you are fat or bald, if you are in your pajamas or in your formal clothes. Once they love you, they love you unconditionally and at the risk of their lives.

And, what do we do? We want them to be gathered and taken away from, we don't want to see them, and we say excuses. Then, I am asking to those who act like that, do you know that the neighborhood you currently live in was belong to the cats and dogs which you have just thrown out. If you want let's try something else. Dear animal despiser, you make a list of to-be-exist and not-be-exist living beings so that the Noble Creator creates according to your list. What do you say?

No matter what you say the world is both yours and them. If you breathe they will breathe too, there is no other way of it. It is the rule of God. All living beings have a right to live.

Dear pet lover or don't-lover friends of mine, let's declare tomorrow as a making pets happy day and let's feed at least one living being. With anything you have at home, anything you can afford. When it eats, observe it and feel the unconditional love coming from it to you. Feel it inside of you and don't forget to thank. Thank, because of its presence today to make you achieve your intention.

Tame love = unconditional love. If you meet it, believe me it is priceless. Why don't you try? ☺

HI, ARE YOU AVAILABLE? YOUR SOUL IS CALLING

It is good to be called, isn't it? Being able to be called and being concerned by others. Are you the one who is called frequently? Do you answer the all calls or is your phone-line busy? Let's think about it.

Our souls always call us, they call us every day but we are either not available or the line is busy. Then, what should we do to be available when our souls call us? First of all we should become clean of the yesterday's regrets and tomorrow's anxieties. If we just focus on this moment, the line wouldn't be busy. Because the reason of the busy tone that your soul hears anytime it calls you is you have anxieties, worries, fear, desperateness, hopelessness and loneliness in your intelligence. Your soul's ability to reach you directly is possible with peace and confidence.

What if you don't hear the phone ring or you are not at home when it calls? If you send this message from your hearth to your soul, I am sure your dear soul will reach you anytime it calls: My dear soul, I want so much to reach you and communicate with you so, please make contact with me and make me feel your presence. From now on, my receivers are always on 'on-mode' to receive every call of you and I love you my dear soul.

Now, the only thing you should do is wait to be called, relax and trust the fluency. ☺

THE BAZAAR OF SENSATIONS

Do you like bazaars? I do but I don't find time to go to except the bazaar of sensations. Today we can wander in the bazaar of sensations as much as we want and I hope it will be useful for each of us.

Now, visualize yourself in a bazaar but it is a bazaar which people greet each other with smiling faces, nobody tries to sell something by shouting and is decorated with colorful flowers. It is a wonderful place that takes you under its influence immediately. Let's skim over the stands to see what is on there. Here are the stands; indulgence, love, respect, affection, joy, peace, wisdom, goodness, optimism, friendship and unconditional love. Now, you can take anything you want, from any stand you want, as much as you want. Stroll the stands slowly, don't hurry. When get back to the home, if you realize that there are things you forgot to take, don't be sad.

Don't forget, bazaars are set up every week. You can take your deficient next week. Have a good bazaar day. ☺

TAKE OUT YOUR SOUL TO SHOPPING

Shopping is good, isn't it? Shopping is actually the repetition of giving and taking actions. Everybody go for shopping but the limit is indicated through budgets. Is there any place or time you can shop unlimitedly?

Of course, there is. Take out your soul to shopping and shop as much as you want without concerning about money.

Now, close your eyes and lie down where you can never be disturbed. Stay as you are for a while and relax completely by breathing deeply. Now, visualize your soul and look at its shape without trying to give a shape to it. No matter which shape your soul is, salute it with love and let it salute you back. After this full of love greeting, take your soul and go for shopping. The rest is up to you. You can buy anything you want, as much as you want because there is no limitation or restriction. First, I buy some indulgence and then some affection and some peace and confidence, of course. I furnish my soul well with these feelings. My soul is so happy and joyful because of the feelings I bought for it. What did you buy? Is your soul as happy as mine too? You can finish your shopping and go back to home anytime you want.

I hope you enjoy taking out your soul to shopping. Come on then, put the feelings in their places before they turn bad, what are you waiting for? ☺

OLD SHOES

The people also want to change but they are also afraid of alteration to death. Even if all the experiences the person has been through are bad and painful ones, the one don't want to leave them behind. Because the old one is familiar one and the one he or she feels safe with it. That is why some people don't want to leave their shoes just like they don't want to leave their old habits, they keep living with them.

How do you feel in this situation? Even if it is old or chafes your foot, don't you leave your old shoes? Or are you one of those who leave the old ones in the minute they buy new ones?

Now, think both of your old shoes and the new ones that you are keeping aside to prevent them from becoming old. Which one is more comfortable? Of course the old one; just like the old habits that you don't actually like and also prevent you from time to time. Then one day you see a pair of elegant shoes at a shop-window, you like them and decide to buy. Just like renewing a habit you have been trying to change. Then you go back to home, but you don't wear the new shoes a lot because the old ones are more familiar and comfortable.

Yet, if you dare to wear the new shoes, who knows what beauties will be included in to your life. What do you think, isn't it the time for you to leave your old shoes behind? ☺

HAND IN HAND WITH GOD

Sometimes we forget that we are not alone and our souls fill with desperateness of the loneliness. However, a person is never alone during the life game. God is always with you anywhere, anytime. Even if you forget him.

If we remember the presence of God next to us, that he always holds our hands in this life stage and never let our hands go in order to make us achieve the best and most beautiful one for us, it will be easier to perceive the life. Because you feel that you are always loved and protected. God's infinitive love and mercy covers us like a mother looking after her baby. The life becomes more meaningful when we remember, feel and mention about him.

So, never forget. You are not alone. You always walk through the life as hand in hand with God. Just remember and feel. ☺

CONCLUSION

Until you came to this page, we have walked through together with you in the journey of creating The Miracles of the Soul. I hope you have started to create your own soul's miracles in your lives, like me. Thanks to each of you. Thank you very much for letting me accompany you through this journey and I love all of you so much.

Just because of you who you are. I send you my best regards with the hope of meeting again at other journeys.

Hope your soul always creates miracles. Stay with love. ☺

PERVİN VATANSEVER